EN BIOGRAPHY OF A DIVORCED MINISTER

ENTANGLED BIOGRAPHY OF A DIVORCED MINISTER

JIM HOWARD

TATE PUBLISHING
AND **ENTERPRISES**, LLC

Entangled Biography of a Divorced Minister
Copyright © 2013 by Jim Howard. All rights reserved.

No part of this publication may be reproduced, stored in a retrieval system or transmitted in any way by any means, electronic, mechanical, photocopy, recording or otherwise without the prior permission of the author except as provided by USA copyright law.

Scripture quotations are taken from the *Holy Bible, King James Version*, Cambridge, 1769. Used by permission. All rights reserved.

This book is designed to provide accurate and authoritative information with regard to the subject matter covered. This information is given with the understanding that neither the author nor Tate Publishing, LLC is engaged in rendering legal, professional advice. Since the details of your situation are fact dependent, you should additionally seek the services of a competent professional.

The opinions expressed by the author are not necessarily those of Tate Publishing, LLC.

Published by Tate Publishing & Enterprises, LLC
127 E. Trade Center Terrace | Mustang, Oklahoma 73064 USA
1.888.361.9473 | www.tatepublishing.com

Tate Publishing is committed to excellence in the publishing industry. The company reflects the philosophy established by the founders, based on Psalm 68:11,
"The Lord gave the word and great was the company of those who published it."

Book design copyright © 2013 by Tate Publishing, LLC. All rights reserved.
Cover design by Rodrigo Adolfo
Interior design by Caypeeline Casas

Published in the United States of America

ISBN: 978-1-62510-442-7
1. Biography & Autobiography / Personal memoir
2. Family & Relationships / Divorce & Separation
13.04.19

CHAPTER ONE

My name is Jim Howard; I have learned in life that serving God is the best way to live, and I shall continue that way. Jesus said, "These things I have spoken unto you, 'that in me' ye might have peace. 'In the world ye shall have tribulation': but be of good cheer; I have overcome the world" (John 16:33, KJV). Somehow, God does permit his children to suffer persecution and tribulations in this world. We must remember, "we don't live in heaven yet" because we are still in this world, where sometimes "every day with Jesus is sweeter than the day before, still will have its misfortunes without end." Living in Jesus and in the earthly world sometimes is a constant struggle, and I know what I am writing about is very scriptural and very everyday living.

The following incidents over the past thirty-some odd years are all a result of sin, and this particular sin was divorce. This short biography is written for Judeo-Christian believers and/or any family-oriented couples that want strong Christian family values in their families and churches. This is written as an unbelievable biography that did happen and may have happened many times but not recognized, and all because of a divorce. For the sake of not embarrassing any person or church, the names are not listed; however, my name is.

I didn't enjoy writing this article, and it is written like a long letter. I was and am a very private person. I don't like my privacy being infringed on. I am telling things that only a very few people know. I do not like telling it. It is humiliating to write about, and I would rather no one knew it. However, this saga that has been swept under the rug long enough may be of help to someone going through a catastrophic trauma when everything looks and is impossible. I have been there!

Being a pastor for twenty years, I witnessed divorces among Christians. I don't know if you would call them out of the ordinary or not, but each had its turmoil. Divorce in general pays its wages and/or its fruits. Whether we believe it or not, "the wages of sin is death" (Romans 6:23, KJV). Paul didn't say, "The wages of 'some sins' is death." However, the scriptures do tell us "there is a sin unto death"; however, we won't go there (1 John 5:16, KJV).

According to Jesus, you can tell a tree by the fruit that it bears if it is good or bad. "A good tree cannot bring forth evil fruit; neither can a corrupt tree bring forth good fruit" (Matthew 7:15-20, KJV).

Divorce isn't a tree; however, it still has limbs that produce fruits that are not good. I did have one lady church member tell me, "I came out pretty good with the divorce." I have heard divorced couples both say, "We both got what we wanted." I have also heard the distressing stories. When both people are pleased with their divorce, does that make the divorce not a sin? When Christians are talking and dealing with divorce, remember we are talking and dealing with what God calls wickedness, and we are talking about what God said he hates. (Genesis 6:1-7:24, and Malachi 2:16, KJV).

What are the fruits of a divorce? The liberal analysts may not see much because it is a well-established part of our civilization; including it is well established in God's churches. Surely not God's churches. Yes, God's churches. Honest, literate ministers of the Gospel will tell you, "Its fruits are not good fruits, and it is wickedness." Often, the children are the victims of divorce, and these range over a multitude of problems. Some divorces have produced fruits of violence, verbal nastiness, and murder. Paranoia plays a big part of cheating on a spouse as well as divorce. I talked to one woman that told me she hid all of her husband's guns because she didn't know what he might do if he found out she was cheating on him. I am sure most of us know by listening to the news the manslaughter charges that have accompanied cheating on one's spouse, including divorce.

Some years ago on the news, I heard about a man in Emporia, Kansas, who was told by a lady that she didn't want to be married to him, and that upset that man very much. He went into the church where this lady went while the service was in progress and just started shooting people.

After that, on the national news, another man that was told by a lady that she didn't want to get married, and it upset that man very much. That man went into a McDonald's restaurant in California where that lady worked and started shooting people.

There is something about love, lust, hate, romance, marriage, and divorce mixed up the wrong way that can bring about very violent, unpredictable situations.

However, I have known Christians that went through a divorce, and regardless of the reason and regardless of who was responsible, today they are serving God and are a blessing in their church and community. We cannot use that as an excuse to sanction divorce. However, we must remember God is a god of love and grace, and the first thing he wants from any sinner, regardless of who the perpetrator is that is responsible for the divorce or any sin, is repentance. A truly repentant divorced and remarried person can be a blessing to God's work, *if* they are truly repentant. Remember, all of us Christians are sinners saved by grace. Sometimes we must repent again, and sometimes when we do repent again, we don't act like it; however, God knows our frame (Psalm 103:14, KJV). But again, some Christians don't act like Christians. We could ask the question: what is a Christian supposed to act like anyway? We all come from different sides of the track, and we accept Jesus as our savior on the knowledge of what we have received and know. God sees the heart and saves the soul from that point of view. In time, a real, sincere sinner convert will start walking with God and learn that the way of the cross leads him or her very close to God, and we see that person as a very godly person, even though their walk with the Lord is much different than ours. Jesus told his disciples, "I have other sheep that are not of this fold" (John 10:16, KJV).

Many Christians are familiar with the story of Jonah. God told him, "Arise, go to Nineveh, that great city, and cry against it; for their wickedness is come up before me."

And many know Jonah didn't want to go because he would just as soon Nineveh be destroyed because of what they had often done to the Hebrew children. So Jonah got on a ship to go elsewhere just to get away from going to Nineveh. A mighty storm arose on the sea and battered the ship, and it seemed all would be lost. After some interrogation, they learn that Jonah was the problem. Jonah told them to cast him overboard and the ship and crew would be saved. Reluctant, they threw Jonah overboard and the storm eased. God prepared a great fish or whale to swallow Jonah. In the stomach of the whale Jonah prayed to the Lord. Three days later, the whale spit Jonah up near land. So, after Jonah became a graduate from "Whale University" he went. We know the story of how Nineveh repented and wasn't destroyed. No matter how bad, big, and wide the wickedness is, God would rather have people repent than to be destroyed. How does repentance have anything to do with divorce? Well, let's just see.

Before the day of Noah's flood, some of what God called wickedness were repeated marriages, divorces, and polygamy. In spite of Noah preaching righteousness, there was no repentance, so the rains and the flood came. They were given time to repent. We must remember that the known world of that day was all wicked, except for Noah and his family.

I have heard so many different remarks on the news about so many divorces, and so little is done about it in spite of what it does to children and all of its violence. Divorce is a problem, and it is contrary to Judeo-Christian principles. It used to be somewhat contrary to our USA principles. Divorce is such wickedness that God said he hated it because it is a sin of violence Malachi 2:16 (KJV): "This violence isn't always on the outside." Sometimes an inner catastrophic trauma is nothing but violence that injures the mind, heart, and soul. Some children have a catastrophic pain down deep in their chest because of what is happening to their world. I know what I am writing about because I have been there. At age eleven, my own son said to my ex and me, "If you get a divorce, I'll hate you both for the rest of my life." I know that was pain talking. Why do couples put pain in their children to talk?

There are times when something goes so wrong in a marriage that the emotional conflict is so catastrophic, divorce is the only solution. I think God could heal a situation like that; however, it takes both parties to surrender to God for that to happen, and usually only one party is willing and maybe neither.

If anyone says divorce is no big thing because we are saved by grace—better be careful because calling God a liar is a setting that you better remember you are the liar, for God can do no wrong.

Remember, divorce and remarriage is the first widespread wickedness that God dwelt with in Adam's race. God spared not the old world but saved Noah, the eighth person, a preacher of righteousness, bringing in the flood upon the world of the ungodly (2 Peter 2:5, KJV).

In Genesis 5:29-7:24 (KJV), we see the picture of Noah, his wife, their three sons, and their wives. This family portrait without divorce and remarriage found favor with God.

After our new country won its independence from Great Britain, we embraced the Judeo-Christian values into our society, courts, and government. In our early days as a new country, not only Christian America but also Americans in general valued the Word of God as God (John 1:1, KJV).

Over the years, Americans—including a multitude of Christians—have accepted the "days of Noah" as being accepted by God all because we are saved by the grace of God. We can do anything we please, and God will forgive us. Paul said, "Moreover the law entered, that the offence might abound. But where sin abounded, grace did much more abound" (Romans 5:20, KJV). Since Paul said that, why should we worry about sin or repent of sin?

Some of our Judeo-Christian society feels as the early Roman Christian society felt; if we sin, it is okay because we are all sinners saved only by the grace of God (Romans 6:15, KJV).

Divorce isn't the only sin that God hates. God hates sin regardless of what sin it is; however, he loves the sinners and sent his only begotten Son to die on Calvary for them (John 3:16, KJV). He also, while on the cross, nailed the handwriting of ordinances that was against us to the tree (Colossians 2:14, KJV). Still, some Christians seem to think God also nailed repentance to the tree. I haven't found any Scripture to support that scenario.

This scripture doesn't get out of date. God said, "If my people, which are called by my name, shall humble themselves, and pray, and seek my face, and turn from their wicked ways; then will I hear from heaven, and will forgive their sin, and will heal their land" (2 Chronicles 7:14, KJV). If you feel this scripture is out of date because we are all sinners saved only by God's Grace, read what God said to the seven churches in Revelations 1–3 (KJV) when they were all sinners saved only by God's grace. Any way we look at it, sin pays wages, and divorce is a sin, and it pays wages; and in my review, it also produces fruits that we would just as soon ignore, and the tragedy is that we are ignoring it (Romans 6:23, KJV).

I have read stories like the following; however, I never thought I would be one of its victims. Even though some divorces may not be so bothersome, according to God's Word, "divorce is still a sin that God hates." This story is hard to believe, but I was there and was a victim and witness of the whole ordeal. To start with, I will insert the words of Jesus: "He that is without sin among you, let him first cast a stone at her" (John 8:7, KJV).

We all, as Bible born-again Christians, have to accept the fact that "all have sinned and come short of the Glory of God" (Romans 3:23, KJV). I am in that category. I am guilty of sin and cannot throw stones. I have repented of my sin and sins, and I know what the accountability of it is. Thank God Jesus paid the debt for my sin and sins on Calvary and my heart and soul have been cleansed; however, "I am still just a sinner saved 'only' by God's grace." It bothers me when some Christians refer to themselves as saints. In the Epistles, the apostles referred to the believers as saints. If someone else calls you a saint, that is okay; however, if you think and call yourself a saint, you need some heaven-sent Holy Ghost Bible teaching. Nevertheless, sinners saved by the grace of God are saints. Be careful how you judge that phrasing.

CHAPTER TWO

As a pastor, I had a godly wife and two godly children. You couldn't find a better wife and children that loved God and were serving him. Being as biblical as I could, I taught from the Bible that a man and his wife should be as one flesh, faithful to God and to each other. My wife even talked about the faithfulness that should be in a marriage. My children were taught and believed that and expressed it in different nonchalant ways.

A man often attended the last church I pastored; he was a blessing in how he could sing specials, lead in prayer, and support the church financially. There are a lot of churches that would love to have such a person with such talent and used of God.

Then came that bolt of lightning from out of the blue; it struck and blew our church, my children, me, and my ministry all to pieces, and it was hard to believe. My "godly wife" got involved with that man, divorced me, and married him. Being in a denomination that frowned on divorced ministers, I left the ministry. Leaving the ministry was one of my biggest sins. The Apostle Paul said, "The gifts and calling of God are without repentance" (Romans 11:29, KJV). At that time and in all the turmoil I was in, I didn't know what else to do. Yes, I sinned against God, and it was a more wicked sin than divorce because I answered the call of God, and when things got rough, I left the ministry. I must have had some of Jonah's frame of mind, and I did get swallowed by some very devastating things that were as big as a whale. I am not even a graduate of "Whale University" yet, and I may be flunking out.

And Jesus said unto him, "No man, having put his hand to the plough, and looking back, is fit for the kingdom of God" (Luke 9:62, KJV). I am dealing with that.

Maybe I should have written, "There are a lot of churches that would not want a man with such talent and used of God"? Was he really used of God? I'll let you answer that. I found out later one of the main reasons he came to our church was to see my ex. Oh, how naive and trusting I was. Once I overheard my ex tell a member of my church, "My husband is a little naive." Naivety can bring about a catastrophic trauma when you have been taught to always give the other person the benefit of the doubt, and I still am faced with that problem. There is no virtue in being naive, but there are some terrible consequences, and I know what I am writing about.

In the past, I had known of situations like mine, and I felt grief for the pastor being put through such an ordeal. Until I was there, I had absolutely no idea what that pastor was going through. I knew God called me to preach his Gospel. I felt I had missed out on what God led me to do. However, when I pastored, I knew I was in the will of God. I wondered what I had done so wrong. I wasn't a perfect Christian, pastor, preacher, husband, or father; however, I prayed and worked at it the best I could. I was faithful to my wife, children, and God. Somehow, my ex didn't see it that way; however, she voiced no misguided pleasure until she met this rather wealthy man that praised her beauty and her perfection. Yes, he was a married man as well, and he had a lovely wife and family, and I knew them and they were all my friends. Later, a lady friend told me, "Jim, sometimes it is your friends that you have to watch." I am trying to learn that.

My district superintendent in the denomination that I was ordained in informed me I must resign from their denomination as a minister if I choose to remarry. He told me this when I hurt the worst from losing a wife. God said, "It's not good for man to live alone"; however, to minister in the church I grew up in I must (Genesis 2:18, KJV). I knew all that before he told me; however, him telling me added more pain to my situation. The feelings of rejection I felt from my ex were bad enough, but the rejection from the church that I grew up in, telling me if I choose to remarry, I must resign from being a minister first, doubled the rejection. I was called to the ministry in that church. But that wasn't the worst of the rejection. I had a feeling God was rejecting me, and I knew that wasn't true. However, knowing that didn't stop the feelings of rejection from God, especially when I prayed and the heavens were brass. I had almost constant feelings of "nothing matters anymore." There is nothing I can do that will correct anything. Praying and believing God wasn't working. Divorce is a catastrophic trauma to a minister of the Gospel that believes living close to God and his Word and close to his wife and family is a must. I felt I was doing that, and I felt my prayers went unanswered or were never heard by God. How could I be such a terrible sinner? And I hadn't done anything that I knew of that put me there. Changing those feelings of rejection by God is a trauma in itself. I felt isolated from everyone and everything, including God. For several years after, I had ups and downs spiritually that were out of my control.

However, I knew the following scripture, though it didn't at the time function in my mind, heart, or soul. Jesus said, "I am with you always, even unto the end of the world" (Ephesians 1:13, KJV; Ephesians 4:30, KJV; and Matthew 28:20, KJV). These scriptures were the only assurance I had from God that he was still with me; however, I had no inner feelings that God was with me, even though I knew I was sealed by the Spirit. I felt my first obligation in life was to love God and serve him. At that time, I felt all of that was blown away. I have learned what spiritual confusion is: you see and believe Jesus through blurred vision, including through a dark glass (1 Corinthians 13:12, KJV).

I have always been an extrovert and loved being around people. I tried to keep up my fellowship with people, but I couldn't handle the multitude of questions about the divorce and leaving the ministry because I am not a chastity person; however, now that is exactly what I am. Not my choosing! I am a family man who became a "marriage reject."

At that time, I had migraine headaches, lived on pain-killers (some narcotic pain-killers, migraine deterrents), and the divorce was a trauma itself to aid the migraines. My first Christmas alone, I spent four days and nights in an apartment with one of those migraines. My son and daughter spent the four days with their mother. I had taken the limit of my pain medication for my migraine and just lay in bed with the pain. An associate of mine mentioned if I would take a little bit of liquor, it would relax me and help ease the pain. After not getting any pain relief, I got up from bed and went to the liquor store and bought some liquor and drank some of it. At different times I tried it over and over; however, there wasn't any pain relief or relaxation with the liquor—just intoxication and high blood pressure. Loneliness, pain, and the feelings of rejection by your wife, church, and God is a real dreadful feeling and were constant anguish that cannot be explained or removed, except in time, and then it lingers.

Years after, I still deal with it. When I mentioned to my doctor about trying some alcohol, he said, "You can't use any amount of alcohol with the medication I have you on," so that was stopped; however, the pain and anguish continued. Of course the pain and anguish continued with using the alcohol. I was in such emotional stress; if I had known how to get some illicit drugs and try them, I don't know what I would have done. I have known men who, when a problem got too big for them, went to alcohol. I thought to myself, *Why would they go to alcohol?* I was sure I would never do that. I have learned there is a "state of confusion" trauma—what you know as good common sense just isn't there, and I have experienced that scenario. Oh, to be free from this inner hell is all that mattered. Some reading this article won't have a clue what I am writing about; however, some will feel that groan deep in their mind, heart, and soul because they have been there.

I am aware there are some women that no man can make happy at any length of time, and some men can't be made happy by any woman. I have known women that went through husband after husband, and still they are anxious. I have known men that have done the same. I don't believe my ex was quite in that scenario because she was a very godly and nice lady, but she was bought by a man that had money to spare. He bought and paid for her; however, I didn't get the money. I did get "to pay" some child support; however, I didn't see that as being an in-home father to my son. Godly people can make mistakes, and I know the negative questions that go with that: are they really godly?

I had gotten a job and managed to maintain it while fighting loneliness, rejection, and migraines, and it was almost unbearable. In time the migraines vanished, but I still fight the rejection and loneliness. Rejection is a bad feeling. Loneliness is a bad feeling. But the following difficulty caused the loneliness and rejection to mushroom into another stage of isolation.

The divorce wasn't the bad thing that happened to me; however, it was the starter. Somehow my ex-wife talking with my daughter convinced her, "If your husband doesn't meet your needs, it is okay to find someone that will." My daughter wasn't married at the time but had a steady boyfriend and/or fiancé. I saw in my ex one dedicated Christian, and I couldn't believe what she conveyed to my daughter in spite of what she had done in divorcing me. Some people, when they make a mistake, say so but don't endorse it. However, when you take your eyes off Jesus, anything can happen, and you may endorse some sin and/or a lot of sins.

When I was alone with my daughter and mentioned to her about the divorce, my daughter said, "When I get married and something is really lacking in my marriage, I would consider a divorce and remarriage." These may or may not be the exact words she spoke, but they are very close. That was such a shocking surprise to me. I had always felt and taught that if you are not sure of God's will in your marriage and you staying put, you are not ready to get married. If you are entertaining divorce in any way, if something goes a little off-center, you better deal with that issue before marriage or call your marriage off. At the same time, I am aware that things can happen after marriage that can change the whole scenario; however, God's Word hasn't changed, and the "Word was God" and still is (John 1:1, KJV). There is nothing wrong with good Christian counseling during marriage problems. However, when one marriage partner has eyes on another sweetheart, counseling is usually not in the cards.

Jesus said, "What God hath joined together, let not man put asunder" (Matthew 19:6, KJV); however, it is constantly done in the times we live. A real tragedy; it is common in our churches. What is the judgment and sentence of taking apart what God put together? It is something you just don't do. Don't tell me I'm wrong; you just try telling God he is wrong from his letter (Bible) that he gave (wrote) to us.

How should we treat the Christian that just divorced their companion for a "later-model companion"? We better be careful here because that Christian may love Jesus as much as you or I. We must be careful how we judge that assessment. Paul said, "Brethren, if a man be overtaken in a fault, ye which are spiritual, restore such a one in the spirit of meekness; considering thyself, lest thou also be tempted" (Galatians 6:1).

Again, that wasn't the only bad thing that troubled my life by the divorce. At the age of eleven, my son quit having a father when he needed one. My ex had convinced him divorce is okay. My son has since grown, married, divorced, and he smokes. A father may do his best to be a father to a son one hundred miles away in a different town and home, but it is just a show with little substance. God intended for the father to live in the home with his family as head of the family. In our society of today with women's rights, "women do not have to tolerate" a husband, thinking and believing "God placed the husband and father as head of the home," and many today don't' tolerate it or respect it, and that includes a lot of Christian women.

I am sure this is why Jesus said, "Moses gave reason man could divorce his wife, because of the hardness of their hearts" (Mark 10, KJV). It is my opinion in our modern times this applies to women as well. "Women also can have a very hard heart".

I can see why God said "For the Lord God of Israel said that He hates divorce, for it covers one's garment with violence, said the Lord of hosts. Therefore take heed to your spirit that you do not deal treacherously" (Malachi 2:16, KJV). If God feels divorce is treacherous and violent, why does man (including Christians) think it is okay? Whether I am right or wrong, I can see divorce in a home where there is physical violence and physical harm. And I can see it in a family where there is constant verbal violence. Either way, you can see some hearts are full of hardness, and it may or may not be the innocent party.

I admire a man that does his best to be a proper father, even when he is not there in the home. I did my best. Other people seeing you doing your best may or may not be creditable to them; however, that doesn't change the definition of their ex-companion trying. I have seen husbands that were so busy their families did miss them a lot. I didn't quite fit into that category; however, I could have misjudged things. I am not perfect and am a long ways from being perfect, but in spite of my imperfections, I prayed and tried to please God and keep my family together long before any upheaval was visible for a sudden upset.

It's my opinion when a married man starts conveying to a woman other than his wife her beauty, talent, and perfection, he is playing with adultery (Matthew 5:28, KJV). This also applies to women doing the same, especially when this is done in secret and done often because it is so much in the moment—highlighted fun. Lust is carnal and worldly fun and a sin.

But as the days of Noah were, so shall also the coming of the Son of man be. For as in the days that were before the flood, they were eating and drinking, marrying and giving in marriage, until the day that Noah entered into the ark (Matthew 24: 37–38, KJV).

My ex and family threw out all my and my church's teaching about a godly marriage. My family okayed the days of Noah, Balaam's doctrine, and what God said to Malachi the prophet about divorce. Thank God we all are sinners saved only by his Grace. I feel confident that my ex and children are cleansed from their sins by the blood of Jesus. I do feel they have repented. Prior to the divorce, they all were very Christ-centered. Divorce is one of the open doors to the broad-way that leads to destruction (Matthew 7:13).

And of course, there is that other scenario; some people get into a situation, and though they know it is wrong, they do it anyway because of the trying chaos and confusion they're in themselves. My family could have fit in that kind of situation. They started out with just a little romance sensation that mushroomed into a lot of sinful chaos.

Often, some form of illicit flirting, illicit sexual thinking, or illicit sexual activity has been a part of what God has asked us to repent of because he called it wickedness. My definition of *sin* is like most Christians' meaning, and that is "missing the mark." My definition of *wickedness* is "don't aim at the mark." God's message of repentance was given in both the Old and New Testament. I haven't read any place in the Bible that the twenty-first century churches of God would be exempt because of God's Grace, but some Christians sure do think so.

Jesus said unto them, "Moses because of the hardness of your hearts suffered you to put away your wives: but from the beginning it was not so" (Matthew 19:8, KJV). How much from the beginning that was not so? This could very well cover a lot of issues. There are things that "God has kept hid" from the beginning (Ephesians 3:9, KJV). We don't have a Bible record of what all happened the first three days that is recorded in the book of Genesis. In the beginning, God created the heaven and the earth. "And the earth was without form, and void; and darkness was upon the face of the deep. And the Spirit of God moved upon the face of the waters" (Genesis 1:1–2, KJV). There is so much hidden here. We won't learn what God has kept secret from the beginning until after the rapture of the church, and then God may silence some things. As Christians, why can't we teach and proclaim what he said in his word that hasn't been kept secret? Also, God hasn't kept secret that he asked his people to repent, and he would be their healer. I believe this applies to us as individual Christians, churches, and our USA. Oh, yes, to the world also.

> My people are destroyed for lack of knowledge because you have rejected knowledge, I will also reject you, that you shall be no priest to me: seeing you have forgotten the law of your God, I will also forget your children.
>
> Hosea 4:6 (KJV)

Somehow the shame in being divorced has vanished, including the shame of divorcing your companion. Of course, divorce isn't the only sin that has lost its shame. Where has the spiritual trauma of sinning against God, including its shame, gone that Christians used to feel? The world used to show some feeling of shame committing some crimes and/or sins, but now anything goes anywhere with whoever and with no remorse.

What did God mean when he said, "Because you have rejected knowledge, I will also reject you, that you shall be no priest to me: seeing you have forgotten the law of your God, 'I will also forget your children'" (Hosea 4:6)? Whether we believe it or not, like it or not, children do suffer for the sins of their parents.

According to his Word, God hates sin and "I am one of those sinners saved only by his grace." I don't know how many times I have heard someone say, "On the best days where we have done our best for the Lord, we are still just a sinner saved by God's grace." The Apostle Paul wrote, "For what the law could not do, in that it was weak through the flesh, God sending his own Son in the likeness of sinful flesh, and for sin, condemned sin in the flesh" (Romans 8:3, KJV).

God's definition and/or approval of sin, wickedness, or just plain missing the mark is so much different than ours. Not just the world; this includes Christians okaying sin, and they know God will overlook their sin without repentance because they are saved "only by the grace of God." We as Christians have abused this scripture "Believe on the Lord Jesus Christ and you shall be saved" by ignoring other scriptures and not following to where Jesus is leading us (Acts 16:31, KJV).

Jesus said, "Woe unto you, scribes and Pharisees, hypocrites! For ye pay tithe of mint, anise and cumin, and have omitted the weightier matters of the law, judgment, mercy, and faith: these ought ye to have done, 'and not to leave the other undone'" (Matthew 23:23, KJV). At times we would like to hang on to one or two little scriptures to prove our position; however, we miss the whole message from God's Word.

When it comes to any kind of sin that involves any kind of illicit sexual activity, God asked for repentance, not to sanction because of his grace (Revelations 1–3, KJV).

Let's remember, it doesn't matter how many times one has been divorced and remarried; Jesus died for their sins (John 3:16, KJV). Jesus told the women taken in adultery, "Neither do I condemn thee, go and sin no more" (John 8:7, KJV). Can we commit or live in adultery and know Jesus won't condemn us? We better remember Christ's un-condemnation was "go and sin no more."

The woman at Jacob's well was married and divorced five times and living with a man she wasn't married to. Before Jesus dealt with her sin, he offered her living water to drink. The woman said unto him, "Sir, give me this water, that I thirst not, neither come hither to draw" (John 4, KJV). She became a missionary to her village. Did she repent? How could anyone get a good taste of "God's Living Water" and not repent? I am aware of Christians doing just that today; however, are these getting a real spiritual thirst quencher of living waters that Jesus offered the lady at the well? That is something to think hard about. How much of an experience with God are people getting when they go forth in a church service and accept Christ as their savior?

There are seemingly traumas down deep in a soul, unbeknown to the rest of the church, a Christian life is hurting so bad; that soul just loses sight of Jesus, and they trip and fall. It is my feeling the story about the woman taken in adultery fit that scenario, and of course, that is just my two cents. Some people flirt with sin just for the fun of it, and I am afraid that also includes some Christians. If you are flirting with sin, it's because you have taken your eyes off Jesus, You may trip and fall, and that fall could produce some severe emotional, physical, spiritual injuries, and mainly your testimony.

When I think about the Christians that are divorced and remarried so many times, I wonder what will happen when they stand before the Judgment Seat of Christ; they (or we) will not be judged by our feelings of approval or disapproval of what we call sin or what we call saved by grace. All Christians will be judged by their works and the Word of God, and this includes what God calls wickedness, what he calls carnality, and what he calls love of the world down deep in hearts. This also includes what he calls "lukewarm-ness" and loss of our first love (Revelation 2:4, KJV).

One thing is for sure, if we have really been born again, we have a good fire insurance policy because our works will be burned, but we still will make it to heaven (1 Corinthians 3:15, KJV). However, that is taking a terrible chance with our soul, thinking we have a born-again fire-proof insurance policy. Christians living an ungodly life may send their children, friends, and associates to a devil's hell.

We have Ponzi schemes today where people have invested dollars and are proud of their investments, but when they tried to cash in, they had nothing but a lot of empty papers. People who feel they have a good fire insurance policy against hell may have a catastrophic spiritual Ponzi scheme awakening at "the Great White Throne of Judgment." How many people who call themselves the people of God just have a spiritual Ponzi scheme that will last for eternity? Be careful how you judge that concept. Jesus said, "Not every one that saith unto me, Lord, Lord, shall enter into the kingdom of heaven; but he that doeth the will of my Father which is in heaven" (Matthew 7:21).

I am also concerned about my stand before the Judgment Seat of Christ. How carnal and worldly have I been in serving God? I am working on that; it takes a lot of praying and yielding your heart and soul to God to do such. Sometimes that praying and yielding to God will bring a lot of tears that will be hard to control.

Which is worse, or are they the same before God? Married and divorced over and over, or living as whores and whoremongers constantly? I know one answer in behalf of several marriages and divorces; at least they are trying "if" that is the case.

When I think of my situation, I ask myself, *How could a godly wife do such?* Then I answer myself, *Godly people live in a body with a sinful nature, which biblical Christians refer to as the Adamic sin.* We could call it the carnal nature. We could call it the worldly nature. Whatever we call it, it is in our flesh, and who is without sin? When we all get to heaven, just ask King David, who really loved God, if he ever had a man killed so he could steal his wife. I did better than Bathsheba's husband; however, I felt I was being killed more than anything else.

It took some time, but I finally did realize I had made promises to God, and I failed to keep them, though I tried, and I was just as guilty before God. However, I didn't make plans and entertain activities along the way to break a promise that I know of.

Earlier I mentioned Jesus said, "He that is without sin cast the first stone." It is clear to read: I have just thrown a whole wheelbarrow full of stones, so let's talk about my sins, and I should be stoned. Don't worry; I'm not going to list all of them. This low-priced computer may not have enough gigabytes to handle a fraction of them. My ex's biggest complaint was I didn't spend enough time with her. I had heard other wives say something similar at times to me about their husbands not spending adequate time with them. Maybe this is a common grievance among wives. At that time, I couldn't see that, even though my ex aired it several times. How valid is a complaint like that? It may or may not be valid, but it could be an angle to get more attention. Sometimes that is difficult to judge.

Considering the days we are living in, so many families have no father or mother, grandparents are raising the children, some children are even raising their own children, and me saying, "I was a better husband and father than a lot of husbands and fathers" still isn't saying a whole lot, but it does say something!

I was always trying to find ways to make things better for my family. Maybe I did try the wrong way; however, I did try. The scripture reads, "But if any provide not for his own; especially for those of his own house, he hath denied the faith, and is worse than an infidel" (1 Timothy 5:8, KJV). I tried my best to provide for my family; however, what was I not providing for them when I was trying? Was it something that could cause me to deny the faith and make me worse than an infidel? I felt like I had denied something or I was denied something, but what? Did I fail to provide quality time?

I had preached a sermon concerning redeeming the time because the days are evil (Ephesians 5:16, KJV). Not spending proper time with my family, I learned, was and is evil. What could I have avoided if that was the issue?

1. Not necessarily, but most likely, a divorce could have been avoided. I am aware some good mothers and wives can be bought by a man with money, even when everything is fine until those handsome romantic dollars show up on her doorstep with a big smile and praises without end. I also have witnessed this in other family situations. I think the case may be the man doesn't have to be good-looking, young, and dashing; however, if he is parading with money in his back pocket or bank account, he is a beautiful and dashing prince. Money can turn a frog-faced old man into a handsome young prince quicker than him being kissed by a beautiful princess. Don't ask me where I got that, because I think you know!
2. My wife most likely wouldn't have convinced my son and daughter divorce is okay.
3. My son would have had a father as a role model in the home to follow, and this would most likely have avoided him trying smoking, getting married under the conditions that he did, and then choosing divorce.
4. I wouldn't have been a victim of a violent crime. Here's why: I went to see a lady that declined a man's marriage proposal. This man started stalking her. From the evidence we collected, he wasn't going

to let any man near her. I went to see her, and he was patrolling her house and driveway, parking up the street, watching her house and driveway, and/or just driving by. I didn't know that when I drove into the driveway. As I was getting out of my car, he ran and hit me with his whole body, knocking my buttocks into my car door opening, kicking my shins with one of his feet and then the other. My head and shoulders went over the top of the car door opening, and the back of my shins went hard against the lower car door opening. I was incapacitated so fast I had no defense. He grabbed my right hand, wrist, and arm, twisting it into a deformed condition, and threw me down on the cement drive on my tail bone, back, and elbows that caused internal injuries as well as sending me the hospital. My injuries were many crushed disks in my back, a bruised tailbone and prostate gland, a damaged bladder, and a mangled right hand, wrist, and arm. My doctors and the social security disability office diagnosed me 100 percent physically disabled. It cost me my job and all its benefits, such as wages and major medical, life insurance, and retirement benefits. I wrote a one-hundred-page manuscript about the crime; however, none of it is in these few pages. When a man starts stalking a woman that he says he loves, there is something wrong with that man and what he calls love. Stalkers can be very dangerous people. Being a victim of a violent crime is a trauma in itself; however, the following is worse than the aggravated battery crime and the divorce all put together. Most of my associates, peers, and friends know about the divorce and crime; however, the following I have kept very secret because of what it did to me emotionally because I wanted to die. I even kept this from my doctors.

5. About twenty to thirty years after my divorce and also about ten years after the crime, someone told my son and daughter that I abused them sexually approximately twenty to forty years ago in their younger days. I wasn't given any dates. Neither one of my children could remember a time that ever happened. The one who told them that said, "Your father won't remember any of it either because all three of you were so traumatized by the ordeal, all of you had a mental block that blocked out all memory of it." This person told them, "Confront your dad with it. If he denies it, don't have any dialogue with him until he has had therapy and the memory comes back and all three of you deal with the issue."

CHAPTER THREE

It wouldn't be proper to put myself into the same class as Joseph the son of Jacob, but I will use his example. Joseph was accused of attempted rape and sent to prison. At least I didn't go to prison for something I didn't do.

However, I was already in prison. Being the victim of that violent crime, I had already been given a life sentence put behind visible physically deformed body parts and financial bankruptcy, which became bars of confinement. I was deliberately made to be permanently confined in this prison for the rest of my life. I am limited to where I can go because finance and physical disabilities control all travel anywhere. The following went over and over in my mind. Being accused of something I knew nothing about and being real confined to where I couldn't do anything about the accusations, again I felt "God, you—like my ex, church, and children—also have rejected me."

Again, from another situation I was living in, rejection and now more isolation, and it was a mental and spiritual prison or hell. I felt dirty and like an outcast from society, and there was no way out and no place to hide if I could get out. Being a marriage reject is very painful, but the accusation that I abused my children sexually when they were young kindled suicide notions. Now I am a family reject, marriage reject, and a church reject. Keeping this quiet and not talking about it was painful; however, the thoughts of talking about it were more painful. I told very few people, and it was difficult. You may be a man that doesn't cry; however, when you are accused of raping your own children that you love dearly, you will cry. Your love for them will tear your heart apart. And sometimes your crying will be uncontrollable. Writing this has brought tears, and sometimes I have trouble turning them off; however, writing about it is easier than talking about it. I can take time out from writing and compose myself, whereas by talking—that would be more difficult. Hiding these thoughts and feelings was poison to my mind, heart, and soul. I knew I needed to talk about the accusations, but it was too painful. It was difficult to talk to the few people that I did talk to. I asked them not to spread it around; however, I don't know if they did or not.

I don't know how many times I thought, *God, why have you forsaken me? God, physically I'm not able to do anything, and financially I can't hire a lawyer. God, why?*

You talk about confinement and no visitors; I was and still am in this prison. When you lose your wife and kids, you have lost the big part of your life, especially when you are confined without any visits from them. Losing my wife through a divorce was difficult; it took time, but I got over that. However, losing my children by them being brainwashed by an incompetent analyst or quack is excruciating pain.

When two different people—your own son and daughter—accuse you of raping them, that will do something to you. This is the *hell* you will face. You are damned if you did, and you are damned if you didn't.

Feelings of rejection and isolation are a catastrophic trauma. If my ex and children had been killed in a car wreck, I don't think I would have hurt so badly. Losing them in a car wreck couldn't have been the hell they are putting me through. At least my church wouldn't have rejected me. My brothers and sisters were great, but they couldn't replace my own, the ones that God gave to just me; of course, my kin didn't know all I was going through. One sister did know. I kept the trauma and feelings of it to myself and always acted like everything was okay. Keeping my feelings to myself was bad. I learned to smile and be cheerful with a broken heart, and I have learned a broken heart does not mend by thinking positive and being cheerful. I tried praising God when I didn't feel like it, and that didn't heal a broken heart, and that didn't bring the presence of God.

During all of this time, other medical problems arose such as infections, atrial fibrillation (a heart rhythm problem), and kidney failure that put me in the emergency room, intensive care unit, and hospital many times. Also during all this time, I had to move from my trailer house to a government-subsidized apartment complex for health reasons. I had to make a lot of changes that were financially costly; however, I was better off, though much more poor.

Some people often ask me, "How are you, Jim?" Being I was up and around when so many my age and younger couldn't get out and around at all, I would say, "Okay." I sure wasn't well, but I was okay. When I can, I do my best to get out each day and shop for what I need. My only freedom is around town and sometimes doctor's appointments in Tulsa, Oklahoma, Bartlesville, Oklahoma, Joplin, Missouri, or any close vicinity. I have told very few people of my ordeal. Three ministers here in Montgomery County, Kansas, know some of it. My doctors know some of it but very little. I had often preached, "If something is really bothering you, you need a good listener." I had preached that, but how could I practice it when I wanted to die?

Again, my extrovert personality has turned much more to being very introverted because I have an awkward time talking about any of my past. I changed churches several times, and I found a church to go to that would tolerate me, without asking a lot of questions and not asking me to do a lot of things.

I keep to myself to not deal with questions that I can't answer and to stay sane. Living under such a load is difficult. I do get out of my apartment several times a day for breaks from this small apartment and my computer. I have told some of the tenants I was taking a break from my prison cell. Some of the other tenants have told me the same about getting out of their prison cell. These are very small apartments we live in. I work at being cheerful. I sometimes tease some of the other tenants just for their interaction, reaction, and my sanity. I have found, being many of the tenants here are born-again Christians, that a little quick break is very helpful to a troubled heart and soul. No, they have no idea what I am going through. Anyway, I don't think they do. I put on a very good front. I don't think I am a hypocrite; however, sometimes I am very hypocritical. I dress like I always have; however, my clothes are very old, tattered, and expensive to keep up and usually I have no money to keep them up. I dress very causal around the apartment complex. I have learned what it is like buying some clothes at rummage sales, and for me that is embarrassing. I have learned I am not as proud as I used to be; maybe God is working on my pride as well.

I write to stay sane and somehow hope to develop an author profile. However, hardly knowing an adverb from a proverb and good sentence-structure—writing isn't my best skill. I am dyslexic, and reading is very difficult, and I read very slowly. Over the years, I have gotten some books published, but without money to advertise, they didn't sell, and I went into a hole financially that was hard to get out of on Social Security disability pay.

I have learned one of the best ways I could keep my sanity is to write what I feel God has laid on my heart, and I usually feel it deep in my soul. The paradox with this is sometimes I fight feelings of rejection, loneliness, and isolation at the same time I feel God putting things into my heart to write.

There are times I slip in and out of periods of isolation; however, that doesn't last very long. But it is a very good emotional break, even though it's only a few minutes to an hour, and a few times it has been for a few weeks, but it never stays. It usually is a constant battle of ups and downs. Sometimes at church, I feel the presence of God while people are worshiping; however, when church is over, that feeling is gone. Sometimes I listen to Daystar and Bill Gaither's music on the Internet and find it very uplifting. At times I'll have an encounter with a person that is very uplifting because it deals with the present—not the past—and humor.

However, the Apostle Paul said, "Brethren, I count not myself to have apprehended: but this one thing I do, 'forgetting those things which are behind,' and reaching forth unto those things which are before, I press toward the mark for the prize of the high calling of God in Christ Jesus" (Philippians 3:13, KJV). I have preached that to my congregations, but how do I practice it? I wish I could forget. At times I thought, *Alzheimer's may not be such a bad thing.*

However, with me, I would forget the wrong stuff, so I pray I don't go there.

When able, I get out and walk—doctor's orders—but I would do that anyway. When able, I walk because walking makes me feel good. When I go to church, sometimes and often I leave early because of medical problems I received from the crime, and sometimes because of my a-fib heart condition. Sometimes I leave because the anguish of isolation overwhelms me when I get around a lot of people. How can you feel isolation when you are with a lot of people you know? I don't know, but I do, and sometimes it does overwhelm me. Sometimes when I get ready for church and walk out the door, I get overwhelmed with feelings that I can't face the people at church and go back into my apartment. Sometimes when I feel this crowd frustration, I just go for a drive. With the price of gasoline, I am doing less of that.

I am limited in what I can do physically; however, I have learned if I take my time, there are more things I can do. The problem with that is without money, you are really limited. I understand the term *poor farm*. I'm sure that is where I live, and if God doesn't intervene, I'll die here. I drive a very old car, but it runs great, and everything on it works.

Very few people even know anything is wrong. Occasionally, someone will ask, "What is wrong with your right hand, wrist, and arm?" I usually tell them, "I was a victim of a violent crime." Sometimes they probe for more, and I say as little as possible. Most all my doctors know the divorce and crime story. The things that are killing me; I haven't told them. I have several doctors keeping me together and breathing. My a-fib heart condition didn't start until after my children were told I raped them and they told me. I have wondered if the trauma of being accused of sexually molesting my children had anything to do with my a-fib. When my a-fib couldn't be controlled by medication, my doctors put in a heart pacemaker. Some doctor bills have been turned over to collection agencies because I didn't have the money. I have wondered if being turned over to collections had anything to do with my a-fib. I do have Medicare; however, the state is paying my Medicare premium and my Medicare D. However, that doesn't take care of unpaid doctor's bills.

I have been asked why I didn't date. I would respond I can't afford it. Sometimes I'll try to put some humor in it and say, "I'm too young, and my mommy won't let me." I have learned to make things as cheerful as possible in just about everything I say and do. But at the time my children told me what they had been told proved to be a catastrophic trauma in itself to me, and I wanted to die because of the hidden nightmares it has put deep in my mind, heart, and soul.

At that time they told me, I hadn't heard of any false-memory syndrome and/or false memory being programmed into a person by drugs, hypnosis, or just plain brainwashing.

My son and daughter had this therapy, and a false memory was programmed into both their minds, and it traumatized them both. How could all of that happen and no one knew anything about it until some twenty to forty years later, when a person that didn't know any of us invented it by error or just wanted money from fleecing would-be counseling victims that may or may not have a problem? I still don't know how all of this came about; however, my son is beginning to come around some. He doesn't want to talk about it.

From what I have heard on the media, read, and what I have been told, when a person realizes they were programmed with something that didn't happen, that false memory still traumatizes them, and that remains in their thinking and emotions for the rest of their life. The real bad thing is the "trauma of false memory" is far more traumatic than if the situation had happened and dealt with at the time, so I have read, been told, and can see that. The quack analysis emphasizes the false memory so large it becomes a huge monster and destroys stability in the person he is programming.

This false memory implanted into their minds traumatized me more than the divorce, my ex teaching my son and daughter divorce is okay, and the violent crime all put together. After the divorce, I felt nothing mattered anymore. However, because my children were being convinced I abused them sexually in their younger days, my life didn't even matter anymore. I wanted to die, and I came close to ending my life I don't know how many times; however, after several years of it echoing in my mind and praying, I did get over the suicide feelings. You talk about rejection, loneliness, and isolation? My wife divorced me, a felon disabled me physically and financially to where I am confined to staying very close to home, and my children are estranged from me for something I don't know anything about, except what they were told to tell me "that is rejection, loneliness, and isolation in a prison with no visitors." Getting out each day that I could and mingling with society doesn't change the inner hell; however, staying in was and is worse.

Something very unusual started happening. I don't know why, but some very young boys and girls started running up to me and giving me a real quick hug. Some of these were in the churches where I went, and some lived down the street from where I lived and often did my walking. Their little, quick hug was a healing ointment on a lonely broken heart. Some of these youngsters were just kids, and some were in their teens when they started this quick hug-and-gone thing. No, I never told them the blessings they gave me. How could I? The only reason I could come up with, the ones that gave me that little hug and gone, were youngsters that I had often talked to, listened to, and sometimes teased in an area that they seemed to like. Good communication when you are not well sure does bring about touches of healing.

I begin to identify with what Jesus said in Matthew 10:36 (kjv): "A man's foes shall be they of his own household." I have seen families where one person would be saved and the rest of that family gave them difficulty. My family was all serving God, and they were blown every which way as well as blowing me away over something that no one knew anything about until it was dreamed up, invented, and driven deep down into my mind, heart, and soul to imprison me deeper, and they did a very good job of it.

Was my family really serving God when they did all of this to me? Often, good Christians have made bad mistakes, repented, and went on serving God. Jesus said, "I say unto you, that likewise joy shall be in heaven over one sinner that repents, more than over ninety and nine just persons, which need no repentance" (Luke 15:7–10, kjv). I feel repentance has had its place in my ex-family. I pray and believe that it has.

In my very young years, I had developed some very sturdy, heartfelt, godly convictions from home and church teachings that a man's wife and family were precious treasures. What I considered most vital and treasured the most in life were all blown to pieces. Godly convictions can thrill you or kill you. You will think you're being killed when you have been falsely accused of something you know nothing about, when the whole scenario doesn't even fit into your character.

Why didn't I give my wife the time she asked for? Scripture after scripture went through my mind. James said, "My brethren, count it all joy when ye fall into divers temptations" (James 1:2, KJV). Am I being tempted to forget about being called to preach the Gospel and maybe forget about God altogether? Who would listen to me preach? I couldn't keep my own family together; why would anyone want to listen to me preach the Gospel? My own family didn't accept the Gospel of Christ that I preached, or they accepted it and then threw it out. There is something seriously wrong with a minister of the Gospel of Christ that can't pastor because he can't lead and keep his own family together in serving God. I am one of those ministers put out to pasture. It isn't a good feeling because you know somewhere you have failed God but just not too sure where or how.

Then there is that other similarity; God may need this story to help someone else, therefore he permitted it. Sometimes the unheard of needs airing and may not be as unheard of as we think.

I am conscious if I had given my ex what she asked for that might not have stopped that man from offering her "prosperity on a silver platter" to get her. However, it would have taken some blame away from me. But it wouldn't have kept me in the ministry if I remarried. I am aware there are Christian wives that can be bought by a man who has money to entice her, regardless of her first-class role model status in life as a Christian. I believe my ex had a first-class role model status as a Christian; however, a first-class role model status in life as a Christian doesn't put you above sin when money distracts your eyes off Jesus. Money beautifies a lot of sins, just ask any prostitute.

What's the difference in a woman selling her body sexually to a man for money and a women selling out her testimony by a divorce to marry a man with money, or are these the same thing? Think on this: each one is getting and giving to a man and from a man with money being "the interchange."

Some Christians love money just as much as they love Jesus or their companion, especially when there is a lot of praise that comes with the money. Often the grass on the other side of the fence is greener, if there are plenty of greenbacks in his back pocket to make it greener. Sometimes the grass just looks greener but isn't, and we have to break the fence down anyway just to see. A lady friend of mine that had been married several times a while back told me, "Oh, that marriage didn't last either." Evidently, the grass wasn't greener there either.

There is something about money when it shows up on your doorstep with smiles and praises, some Christians no longer see Jesus. No wonder the Apostle Paul said, "The 'love of money' is the root of all evil" (1 Timothy 6:10, kjv). By the time they have gotten their eyes back on Jesus, they are divorced and remarried. When Peter took his eyes off Jesus and began looking around, he began to sink into the lake (Matthew 14, kjv). I have thought, *Could I have gotten my eyes off Jesus and that is why I am sinking in this lake or prison?*

It doesn't matter the reason; however, when Christians lose sight of Jesus, they are open to missing the mark, and they don't know what they may do. Outside of Jesus, we have absolutely no righteousness, and we are at the mercy of Satan, and Satan has absolutely no mercy.

I talked with one divorced woman whose husband divorced her and married a woman that had wealth. I just recently received another letter from a lady that told me her husband divorced her and married a woman with money. Money seems to have a language all its own, and most people understand it. However, I have seen married men trade their good wife for a more exciting, younger, prettier, wealthier, and thinner wife. Maybe the reason their exes got so boring, old-looking, not as pretty, and fat is because of whom they had to live with. However, this also applies to ladies that trade off their good companion for a more exciting companion with or without money. There are, more often than not, two sides to every family's turmoil.

Let us use the word *loneliness* here. Those that trade off their companion for a more exciting companion, for money or no money, is it because they are married and lonely—or both? That is something to think about. Maybe I just wasn't exciting, and my ex was lonely. Regardless of the situation, with some people, if money is involved, nothing else matters. I had one lawyer tell me about our court system, "The man with the money buys the verdict," and how often is that true? With some people, money becomes their force, and they do as they please to get it or to buy something with it, even if what they purchase belongs to someone else.

Paul said, "In everything give thanks: for this is the will of God in Christ Jesus concerning you" (1 Thessalonians 5:18, KJV). It has taken me time to consider this is the will of God in Christ Jesus, yet scripturally it must be. I have a hard time saying scripturally it is; however, I must say it that way, whether I see it or not, for it is God's Word.

Peter said, "It is better, if the will of God be so" that you suffer for well doing than for evildoing (1 Peter 3:17, KJV). What was I doing so well? I was preaching the Gospel, and of course, that is well doing—that is, if I did it well. However, could I be suffering for evildoing? Not giving my wife the time she asked for may have been evildoing, and I know I am crowding the issue here because giving her what she asked for may not have changed anything where money was involved. What's wrong with a preacher's wife divorcing her husband that was a pastor of a church to marry a millionaire anyway? God's Word is pretty clear on that.

In Galatians 6:9 (KJV) and 2 Thessalonians 3:13 (KJV), the Apostle Paul said, "Let us not be weary in 'well doing': for in due season we shall reap, if we faint not." How do you not faint? I am dealing with all that, and often I am emotionally and spiritually faint. Not giving my ex the time she asked for, I was suffering for evildoing. That is hard to admit, and it has taken me a long time to even see it, if that be the case! I did try to give her what I could. Was I any more wrong in not giving my ex the time she asked for compared to other husbands and fathers that have been accused of the same? I just don't know.

I have talk to men and women both who have told me their companion asked them to do something for them just to please them, and when they did it, their companion complained anyway. If I had given my ex what she asked for, would she have said, "You should have given more" or at least hinted such? Again, I just don't know.

I have wondered if all men and women are plagued by an underlying feeling that just craves more attention than what they are getting from their companion. Could that be just a normal desire? That's worth thinking about.

CHAPTER FOUR

"Beloved; think it not strange concerning the fiery trial which is to try you, as though some strange thing happened unto you" (1 Peter 4:12, KJV). I had preached that, but how do I practice it?

Paul said, "There hath no temptation taken you but such as is common to man: but God is faithful, who will not suffer you to be tempted above that ye are able; but will with the temptation also make a way to escape, that ye may be able to bear it" (1 Corinthians 10:13, KJV). I am still not sure I can bear it. Many times I thought God was making a way for me to be free from this confinement but all seems like a brick wall with steel bars over the windows.

In the Apostle Paul's dilemma, God said to him, "My grace is sufficient for thee: for my strength is made perfect in weakness" (2 Corinthians 12:9, KJV). Then Paul said to the Corinthians, "Most gladly therefore will I rather glory in my infirmities, that the power of Christ may rest upon me." I couldn't see God's grace being sufficient for me, and I know that is negative thinking. I am still looking for a place for glory in this prison that I am in. If people don't think you being tied down to a small government-subsidized apartment and local area and being physically and financially impoverished is a prison have never been there, and I live here. Again I am wrestling with "What can God do with my weakness?" Remember, God said, "My strength is made perfect in weakness." I am dealing with that.

While pondering my situation, I think of the Christians who are confined to a wheelchair or a bed and have to be cared for hand and foot. My situation is better than that. My situation is "once having ample," and then everything is taken away—and mostly by my ex-family.

There were times that I said to the Lord, "I don't understand my situation. However, I am going to praise you anyhow." David said, "But thou art holy, O thou that inhabits 'the praises' of Israel" (Psalm 22:3, KJV). Oh, that was hard to do, but I did it I don't remember how many times, and I got nothing from God. I confessed my sins and repented over and over and never received anything from God. I didn't really know what sins I was confusing; I was just trying to reach God. Like the Apostle Paul, I tried to glory in my infirmity, confinement, or prison—whichever word is appropriate—and I felt like a hypocrite because I didn't know how to glory in it. However, according to his Word, God was still with me, though I could not feel or witness it in my mind, heart, and soul in any way most of the time.

David said, "My God, my God, why hast thou forsaken me? Why art thou 'so far' from helping me and from the words of my roaring?" (Psalm 22:1, KJV). David felt isolation from God.

And about the ninth hour, Jesus cried with a loud voice, saying, "*Eli, Eli, lama sabachthani*?" That is to say, "My God, my God, why hast thou forsaken me?" (Matthew 27:46, KJV). Jesus felt this absence or isolation from God, and he was the Word of God, which was made flesh. I get a little comfort from that scripture.

Being confined financially and physically to the extent I couldn't even date removed an outlet to rid loneliness. I tried mixing with some Christian ladies but had nothing to offer them. I was overtaxed with medical problems, medical bills, and sometimes bills that were turned over to collection agencies. I had to fill out charity papers over and over. When you have always worked for your way in life and then put on charity, that is humiliating. I was confronted with bankruptcy many times; however, I kept doing without just to survive, without bankruptcy. I tried counting my blessings I don't know how many times. I tried to consider being alive, having something to eat, something to wear, and saying hi to my neighbors, and them returning it was a blessing. These things are a blessing; however, they are also unique traumas that can blow all these blessings to hell.

I am still trying to figure out what Paul and Peter meant about "fiery trials and the will of God being common to everyone" (1 Peter 4:12, KJV). I had preached that. From 1 Corinthians 10:13 (KJV), I couldn't see what I was going through as very common. I knew a lot of people going strong with smiles on their faces and preaching victory all the way. Where was their fiery trial that is common to man? That old yarn "they didn't deserve a fiery trial" doesn't cut much mustard when you are the one in the fire.

When Shadrach, Meshach, and Abednego were in their fiery furnace, Nebuchadnezzar the king saw a fourth man in that fire that looked like the Son of God (Daniel 3, KJV). I know that God is in this fire with me; however, I only know it from Scripture. Again, Jesus said, "I am with you always" (Matthew 28:20, KJV). Sometimes living by faith is doing your best to hang on by faith. Tying a knot on the end of the rope and hanging on is hard to do when there is not enough rope left to tie the knot in. However, you can't fall off the end of the rope with God holding you, but you sure do have a painful commotion going on in your heart.

When Paul was in prison in Rome, he wrote to Timothy.

> At my first answer no man stood with me, but all men forsook me: I pray God that it may not be laid to their charge. Notwithstanding, the Lord stood with me, and strengthened me; that by me the preaching might be fully known, and that all the Gentiles might hear: and I was delivered out of the mouth of the lion.
>
> 2 Timothy 4:16–17 (KJV)

I have wondered if Paul felt the Lord with him, or if he accepted it by faith alone. However, Paul did say the Lord strengthened him. I know what living by faith alone is. I also know what hanging on by faith alone is. I have peace with God; however, I only have it by his Word. Peace in my situation is a whole different ball game. "These things I have spoken unto you, that in me ye might have peace. In the world ye shall have tribulation: but be of good cheer; I have overcome the world" (John 16:33, KJV). Somehow, God does permit his children to suffer tribulations in this world. Just ask Job, Joseph, the Apostle Paul, and a host of other Bible people.

God said to his people, "Behold, I have refined thee, but not with silver; I have chosen thee in the furnace of affliction" (Isaiah 48:10, KJV). I am trying to understand that scripture. It could be I am so full of impureness that God's furnace of affliction is taking longer than usual to refine me, if that be the case. However, I sure do feel the heat of that furnace of affliction.

When I started hearing about this programmed memory being used to make the analyst money by error or just plain quackery, that at least told me my children didn't dream this up. I don't know how it all started; however, I have wondered if my ex had coached them into something that would have led them to that issue. If that be the case, this would make her sin more appropriate. She could have our children all to herself. She had a right to get rid of a sex pervert in the family. But after realizing they didn't dream this up on their own, this helped me give up my suicide thoughts and start writing about it. However, losing them was and is still painful. I came so close to ending my life so many times because of such mental and physical anguish. At times my body just shock intensely in despair and fear.

This feeling of pain, loneliness, and isolation I could see on my face while looking into a mirror while shaving. I didn't have that look before. Of course, I didn't have these feelings down deep inside me before either.

Was this just more of my imagination? I have seen that look of despair on other men and women's faces. I wondered, *Are they having a fiery trial that is common to man?* Some of these people were my neighbors, peers, and Christians; I spent time with them and heard their agony. Over the past twenty-some odd years, some with that look committed suicide. Was that common fiery trial they were going through that catastrophic? It was "just" cancer. It was "just" bankruptcy. It was "just" complications of old age. It was "just" a divorce. It was "just" a nursing home they didn't want to move into. And on goes today's people tried in their fiery trials. Where does it end? I am still "just" here. We never know what is someone's "just" very common fiery trial is when it could be a catastrophic mayhem. I have wondered at times, maybe God is trying to teach me something about Christian's trials that I have missed, and I am discovering I am a very slow learner.

I am not writing this to cry on anyone's shoulder. However, someone may get help from my experience. I have found writing about my pain kind of eases some of it. I started writing about this many years ago, and my computer had a problem, and I lost the whole file. So I am starting over. My memory of it in my mind wasn't lost in the computer problem. Over the years, I have tried to forget some of it; however, I can't.

After the divorce and the crime, I began losing about everything I had. After the divorce, I didn't have a whole lot left anyway. I did have a good-paying job before the crime, a good, old trailer house, two old but good cars, real good shop, hand and shop tools, a lot of musical instruments, books, and some real nice antiques, and the divorce and the crime cost me just about all of it. Now, I am down to one old car that runs good, and I am thankful for that.

I prayed, "Heavenly Father, you saved me, filled me with your Holy Spirit, and called me to preach your Gospel. I answered your call, I preached your Gospel, witnessed to sinners, visited the sick, and prayed with and for them, paid more than my tithe to you, and did your work. My body is broken, I can't pay my bills, I am alone, and nobody cares." The words of David I felt. David said, "I looked on my right hand, and beheld, but there was no man that would know me: refuge failed me; no man cared for my soul" (Psalm 142:4, KJV). I felt and still feel that isolated. I wondered again and again, *God, why have you forsaken, rejected, or put me out to pasture?* Seeking God for help seemed like vanity. Sometimes I wondered, *God, am I that spiritually lukewarm that you are spewing me out of your mouth?* (Revelation 3:16, KJV). My prayers just went unanswered. That feeling of "I have absolutely no one to turn to for help"; I could not get rid of. When you feel you have been rejected by God, knowing scripturally you haven't doesn't change that mental trauma. I understand a little of what David was going through. That feeling I still can't explain, and at times it still overwhelms me. Praying and believing God just doesn't get rid of the feeling; however, continuing praying and believing may. I think sometimes God is just watching me just to see how I weather this storm. I haven't done a very good job yet.

I have often preached, "Sometimes we must just believe and keep walking when it appears the whole world is against us." I was sure I had practice that. Doesn't practice make perfect? I was trying to figure out how to do *now* what I had preached *then*.

When I walk down the street or in a store, people don't see a man disabled physically, financially, emotionally, and spiritually. I do a real good job hiding it. However, people do see a smile on a casual but fairly well dressed zombie's face. Very few people around me knew or know anything about what I was and what I am going through. In public, I make it a point to be cheerful. When I can't put a smile on my face, I stay home, and I stay home or around home a lot.

I tried to keep up my guitar playing after the crime; however, my back wouldn't permit me to lift and carry very much, so that was stopped. At first, not being able to do much, I gained a lot of weight and got very fat. When my doctor gave me epidural injections in my back to ease a lot of back pain caused from the crime, I finally was able to walk and worked my walk up to fifteen miles a day, and I lost the weight. The walking also eased a lot of the pain I felt emotionally, but it didn't stop it; however, at times it made me feel real good just to be out in the open air and walking. After walking, I did my shopping. To be very sociable, I often teased the checkout clerks. Some would remark to me, "Well, here comes Mr. Ornery." I would reply, "Of course" or something to the effect.

I work at being very friendly and cheerful with everyone but only at a distance. I have absolutely no real close friends because that could become very precarious. Someone real close may ask a question, and I don't know how to answer. I do my best to make my one-on-one meeting with a person or persons as humorous as possible and very short in time and at a great distance from my inner pain. No facts of my past if possible, unless it is something way back before my saga. I try to be in control of every situation that I can. I work at creating the situation because that little crazy interaction does something down deep inside me that eases a little pain. It not only eases emotional pain, but I feel better physically, and I know that is a little unrealistic, but I still notice it.

In my younger days, I had seen some older men talk strange, silly, or just plain crazy to people in different situations. I thought to myself, *That old geezer has misplaced his brain.* I was sure I would never be that silly or bickering. Well, I have become that strange old geezer just to stay sane, and sometimes I think my brain is misplaced.

I have wondered how many people I meet every day who are the most pleasant, but they carry a pain deep inside them like I do that no one knows anything about except God. If I ever get this published, at least some people will realize why I avoid so many groups where there is a lot of talking that includes a lot of questions and why I am so distant. At least I won't have to do much talking with this writing out. I can just say, "Read it." I hope that will work. However, writing about it seems to ease thoughts of talking about it. I don't know how real that will be yet. I hope I can handle it, and I think I can. The more I write about it, the easier it gets and the lesser the pain is; however, it is still there.

Though I had gotten over my suicidal notions, I often would pray at nights, "Father, in Jesus's name, help me go to sleep and let me die in my sleep because tomorrow will be just another today, and I can't stand the long day of loneliness and isolation." Loneliness and isolation are some things that just don't disappear or even go away. I take them to church with me. I have them when laughing with the other tenants here in the apartment complex. I take them shopping with me while kidding with the store personnel. It is an indescribable pain, but people that live with it know it, and often it is something not to talk about, and you learn to live in spite of it, and you proceed daily like everything is perfect.

Through all of that, while wrestling with God, I finally told God what I was going to do, and he had to accept it. I would caution anyone to think twice or three times before praying like I did. I wouldn't advise this in any way; however, I prayed, "Father, I am losing everything I have. My health is battered, I can't get a job, I can't pay my bills, and SRS won't help me. (Later, SRS did start helping me a little.) Father, your Word says, 'If we pay our tithe, you will pour out to us a blessing over abundant.' I have done that plus extra giving, and look at me. Where is that abundant blessing? I did what you asked, and I did it because I loved you, wanted to serve and please you. Trying to love and please you, I have become physically and financially impoverished and an outcast from society! I am not going to pay my tithe anymore because I am in such physical, financial, emotional, and spiritual state, I can't even pay my bills or do anything. Father, the only thing that I can really cling to and give you is my faith in you, and that is very small, but that's all I have left."

I didn't hear any voice, didn't see any handwriting on a wall; however, I felt something deep down in my soul as if God was saying, "And it has taken *me* so long to get you here."

What God dropped deep in my mind, heart, and soul, I had been preaching for twenty-some odd years. Was I living that for that twenty-some odd years? Yes, I was, but with some self-righteousness to go with it. Oh, I was genuinely saved, and I knew it; however, I couldn't understand the situation I was in, being a child of God. Living on charity and Social Security disability is very embarrassing. Maybe God is trying to humble me, and if he is, he is doing a real good job of that.

I grew up in Pentecost, heavily weighted down, with some old holiness teachings. A lot of the teachings were right, but some were in error. However, I had accepted the teachings and the doings and the not doings as part of my salvation. I had one pastor that taught if you do certain things—like smoking, drinking, dancing, going to picture shows, and a host of other things—you backslide and lose your salvation, and if you don't repent, you go to hell when you die. Being very young in giving my heart to Jesus and wanting to love and please God, I bought that teaching and lived that way the best I could.

It had been said about that pastor, when he preached about hell, you see the flames, you feel the heat, and you smell the smoke. Maybe that is saying it a little strong; however, I witnessed it, and it sank deep in my mind, heart, and soul.

Our next pastor emphasized we are saved by the grace of God. I really bought that; however, that old teaching by the last pastor hung on to me. I had committed a "serious sin." I was proud of the way I was living and serving God, didn't smoke, didn't drink, paid my tithe, witnessed to others about Jesus, and was faithful to worship services. When I had done and been all of that, why would God permit my devastation? Doing what I did for God was right, but it was not righteousness or any form of righteousness because the hypocrites in Jesus's day did a lot of that. I knew that I preached that; however, I was glad to relate to people the way I lived. And I know the pros and cons of that position. Pride goes before destruction (Proverbs 16:18, KJV). However, I absolutely don't know if my pride had anything to do with my devastation, but I do wonder.

I wish all young people could have the Christian training that I had in my youth—that through the grace of God, without any strings attached and without any prideful feelings, we are saved. There would be fewer sexually transmitted diseases; fewer young unwed girls having babies;

fewer illegal drug use, and fewer youngsters being killed by a drunk driver, etc.

Jesus said, "So likewise you, when you have done all those things which you are commanded, say, 'We are unprofitable servants. We have done what was our duty to do'" (Luke 17:10, KJV). I am an unprofitable servant, and I have hardly done anything that God has asked me to do. Writing what I just wrote, I am aware I could be a little overreacting with criticizing myself. I am trying to be fair with God and myself, knowing I lack some in being real fair and honest because of not knowing all of God's purpose of this mess that I am and the mess that I am in.

I don't think God deliberately arranged for all of these things to happen to me; however, I do believe he permitted them to happen, and he chose to use them. Again, it would be profane for me to put myself in the place of these Bible men, so I'll just use their example and hope that is sufficient. Remember God permitted Satan to devastate Job to nothing. God permitted Joseph, for no reason but a lie, to be placed in prison, and on goes God's people tried in the fire. And again, I keep wrestling with God regarding the prison that I am in. God was still God when Joseph was in prison, and Joseph was still serving him in prison. God was still God when Job was devastated, and Job was still serving him in all his loss. God was still God when the Apostle Paul was in prison, and on goes God's people in prison when God was still God.

The Apostle Paul said, "But by the grace of God I am what I am: and his grace which was bestowed upon me was not in vain" (1 Corinthians 15:10, KJV). I have often wondered, *Has God's grace bestowed on me been in vain?*

I know I am not much, but I am in one well-built confinement, and God is still God. When some preach "If you really believe, God will deliver you from your prison, sickness, or any kind of devastation," they have no idea what they are preaching. I used to preach that, and I knew what I was talking about was the Gospel, or so I thought. When you have been there, you know differently. I have believed and prayed for years for God's intervention. When we all get to heaven, ask the Apostle Paul, "Why didn't you believe God, and you would have been delivered from that prison?" Say to John the Revelator, "If you had really believed God, you wouldn't have been imprisoned on the isle that is called Patmos" (Revelation 1:9, KJV). Sometimes and often, what we profess becomes a target for Satan to accuse us before God (Revelation 12:10, KJV).

God does some things and permits some things to happen for his glory that we will never understand until we get to heaven. The songwriter C.A. Tindley must have experienced something he just couldn't understand to write "We will understand it better by and by." The songwriter G.A. Young wrote:

> In shady green pastures so rich and so sweet, God leads his dear children along; where the water's cool

flow baths the weary one's feet, God leads his dear children along. Some thro' the waters, some thro' the flood, some thro' the fire, but all thro' the blood. Some thro' great sorrow, but God gives a song, in the night season and all the day long.

Outside of Christ, I have absolutely no song.

Sex offenders have a bracelet with a chip in it so the authorities know where they are at, and they are restricted and monitored to stay away from certain areas. I am not a sex offender, and I am restricted to where I can go and where I can't go because of being a victim of a violent crime and made physically and financially indigent, completely bogged down with no family but a lot of loneliness, isolation, medical problems, and medical bills. Had I not been divorced, I wouldn't have been the victim of that crime.

I had never thought of this before I was put here, but regardless of the prison or what kind of a prison, when you are confined from those that mean the most to you, that is confinement. Other than my ex, I am confined from the family I loved and once had, and they are still out there because they all have estranged themselves from me over something that didn't happen. That is isolation in a sealed prison.

I am down to nothing, and I see a very little Jim Howard; however, I see a great big God, and I keep wondering why I am still down in this prison. God was big when Joseph was in prison. God was big when the Apostle Paul was in prison. God seems to have a lot of experience being a big God when some of his children are in some kind of a mess they can't get out of on their own. I am trying to understand that.

Jesus said, "That ye may be the children of your Father which is in heaven: for he makes his sun to rise on the evil and on the good, and sends rain on the just and on the unjust" (Matthew 5:45, KJV). I am getting rained on and have no place to get out of the rain. I am out in the blistering hot sun and have no hat, umbrella, or shade tree to get under; however, that sun and rain is a good thing to really appreciate as well, and without them, we would have no food or shelter.

There was something about that feeling I got telling God all I had left was my faith in him, and that was very small, that did something deep down in my soul. That little faith I expressed to God secured something deep down in me. That faith-secure position I haven't been able to explain; however, I feel and see it constantly since I prayed that prayer of decision. I see and feel it when I am overcome with isolation and loneliness. John 6:29 (KJV) often probed my mind. Jesus said unto them, "This is the work of God that ye believe on him whom he hath sent." In spite of all the discomforts, I was still doing the work of God by believing God sent his Son to die for my sins. But I could also see what I wasn't doing for God, and that bothered me, even when I considered the isolation I was in.

With those feelings, I said to myself, *God removed Joseph from prison, and God restored Job from devastation.* Then we have Hebrews 11:36–37 (KJV):

> And others had trial of cruel mocking and scourging, yea, moreover of bonds and imprisonment. They were stoned, they were sawn asunder, were tempted, were slain with the sword: they wandered about in sheepskins and goatskins; being destitute, afflicted, tormented.

Hebrews 11:13-14 (NIV)

All these people were still living by faith when they died. (Should we criticize these for not being delivered?) They did not receive the things promised; they only saw them and welcomed them from a distance, admitting that they were foreigners and strangers on earth. People who say such things show that they are looking for a country of their own.

Regardless of how we look at these verses, we must remember, God can do no wrong. God is faithful to those that weather the heat and the rainstorms. My problem is I haven't weathered the storm or storms very well.

I have asked myself, *Where do I fit in those categories?* Then I think the category I seem to fit in is "the imprisonment and destitution." However, people die in prison. I haven't been sawn asunder yet. Maybe I should look for a city whose builder and maker is God and forget about any kind of restoration this side of eternity. However, I have heard preached and have preached, "No matter how the storm continues, keep on believing," and I am doing that.

I used to sing, "I'd rather have Jesus than anything that this world holds today." Though I don't understand my situation, I have complained I wish it wasn't this way, and Jesus is the only person or treasure I have that can't be taken from me. I still wouldn't trade him for what the world holds today. I have learned what tribulations are like in this world, even when Christians are the ones giving me those tribulations, including my ex-family doing their part to aid my dilemma. I still would rather have Jesus than the world without him.

I am concerned on how God is going to handle my complaint. One time Habakkuk the prophet wondered about how God was going to handle his complaint. He said, "I will stand upon my watch, and set me upon the tower, and will watch to see what he will say unto me, and what I shall answer, 'when I am reproved'" (Habakkuk 2:1, KJV). I am awaiting that, and I am sure it will come, and I don't have a clue yet how I will answer.

In all of this, Job sinned not, nor charged God foolishly (Job 1:22, KJV). I have to admit, I have charged God foolishly. Oh, how I have complained! I just don't fit among the saints; however, the mess I am and the mess I am in, I am also a sinner saved only by the grace of God, and I would still rather have Jesus than the world.

I have prayed, "God, I have made up my mind. I'm not able to do hardly anything for you, but here I am. Though I don't understand it, can't see it at all, however, I am very conscious your grace has sustained me, and I am what I am by your Grace."

Though I don't have any evidence of it spiritually, mentally, or physically, I sense with what little faith I have God is watching over me. Don't ask me to explain what I just wrote, because I can't, I just know it.

All of this started with "just" a divorce, and many Christians feel since we are saved by God's grace, the days of Noah are okay, and divorce seems to be rather ideal in God's churches of today. Are they really God's churches? The churches in Revelation 1–3 were all God's churches, and God told them to repent.

I have asked myself, *What would the story of the above be if my ex hadn't divorced me?* I could ask the question this way: what would the story of the above be if I had given my ex more time? However, some people like a new car every now and then, so what's wrong with getting a new companion every now and then? Something new brings excitement, so why not a new companion every few years? After all, the old one is worn out and not much fun anymore. I can't find

Scripture anywhere that saved by grace okays that scenario; however, many of God's people have sanctioned it.

I am so glad that God does forgive us of our sins that he calls wickedness, and we can go on serving him, regardless of where we have been or where we are at; however, he does ask us to "repent and believe the Gospel." Mark 1:15 (KJV) isn't the only place in the Gospel that Christ asks us to repent.

One big question: was I really responsible for that divorce? I am still working on that because some of our naive blunders, including taking our eyes off Jesus just a minute, can bring chaos in wandering far from God.

If a companion (husband or wife) is lacking in being what their companion wants, does that give the other a right to throw out all their wedding vows and divorce them? What is wrong with having a serious talk with each other and working things out? What is wrong with a husband and wife sitting down at a kitchen table across from each other, neither one getting angry or raising their voice, and just talking over disagreements? Jesus said, "Whosoever shall put away his wife, saving for the cause of fornication, causes her to commit adultery: and whosoever shall marry her that is divorced commits adultery" (Matthew 5:32, KJV). I am sure I could have forgiven my ex for her sin; however, I have been wrong before in my judgment.

Thanks for reading my memoirs in *Entangled Biography of a Divorced Minister*.